BECAUSE OF YOU, JOHN LEWIS

THE TRUE STORY OF A REMARKABLE FRIENDSHIP

BY Andrea Davis Pinkney

ILLUSTRATED BY Keith Henry Brown

SCHOLASTIC PRESS ≈ NEW YORK

His name is as bright as the dawn filled with stars.

Tybre Faw.

He wakes with a dream that sets the sky in motion.

Tybre whispers his wish.

I want to meet John Lewis.

I want to shake his hand.

I want to tell that congressman
            exactly who I am.

Me, Tybre.

That beautiful name sings with the music of possibility.

When you're a kid from
Johnson City, Tennessee,
home to the Tweetsie Trail
and a lake called Boone,
when you're a kid
growing up
in the days of Black Lives Matter,
you know the power of hope
that glistens at sunrise.

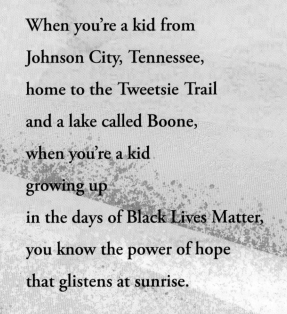

Tybre's grandmothers know it, too.
They pour all their hopes
into that child's future.

In *their* eyes, he is the light
that shines on tomorrow,
while his brilliance flickers today.

When Tybre first discovers his hero,

John Robert Lewis,

friend of Martin Luther King, Jr.,

it lights his dream on fire.

He wants to know the man

who stands for peace and love and truth.

Then, from the pages spring the words

that put wings on Tybre's wish.

John Lewis — all about equality.

John Lewis — unstoppable and brave.

John Lewis — marched across the Edmund Pettus Bridge.

Helped lead six hundred people in the fight for voting rights.

Risked his life on a day we now call

Bloody Sunday — 1965.

Makes that same journey year-on-year,

keeping the memory alive.

John Robert Lewis was a sharecropper's son,
with dreams of becoming a preacher.
He even preached his little-kid sermons
to the chickens on his family's farm.

When you're a boy
in Troy, Alabama,
home to the Dixie Trail,
gospel Sundays,
and gut-bucket blues,
when you're a boy
who has tasted
the bitter fruits of racism,
faith flows
like gold
from a honeycomb.

One Sunday morning, years later,
while John listened to the radio,
the words of Martin Luther King, Jr.
crackled through Zenith speakers.

Who was this man?

Martin — telling the truth of Jim Crow's thorny beak.

Martin — speaking the honest-to-goodness about hate.

Martin — talking of racism.

And standing up against it with peace and love.

Hearing Martin's words lit a light in John's heart.

They flew straight
to John's wide-open hopes
and tucked themselves
into the deepest pockets of his understanding.

I want to meet that clergyman.
I want to shake his hand.
I want to tell Martin Luther King, Jr.
            exactly who I am.

Me, John Robert.

Tybre Faw reads.
And wants. And waits.
He has caught the fire of Martin and John.
Tybre reads it in history books.
John Lewis got the nickname "Good Trouble"
on account of speaking out for what was right.
Tybre reads about John Lewis
at lunch-counter sit-ins, and freedom rides,
and in registering people to vote.
He reads it in the newspaper.
John Lewis brought his own kind of bold
to the House of Representatives.

Every time Tybre reads, he bookmarks,
underlines, folds back, keeps track
of anything to do with the where and when
of the unstoppable Congressman John.

Then comes the day.
Tybre convinces his grandmothers
to pack up their car.
Fill its tank. Stuff the back seat
with a snack box and books.
And make the four-hundred-mile drive
from Johnson City, Tennessee,
to Selma, Alabama,
where his hero will be making
the once-a-year march
across the Edmund Pettus Bridge.

A whole lifetime before Tybre was born,
John Lewis, now a teen, applying to college,
wrote a letter to Martin Luther King, Jr.

Told him — Troy State University is segregated.
Told him — schooling is unfair.
Told him — WHITES ONLY signs everywhere.

John asked Martin what to do
about Jim Crow's crooked croon
in the segregated, prejudiced state of Alabama.
That's when a bus ticket arrived.
Martin Luther King, Jr.
invited John Robert Lewis to meet him.

Martin called John "the Boy from Troy."
And they called each other "friend."

In time, John and Martin came together.
Arm in arm.
Heading in the same direction with
the many men and women in the movement.

From 1960 to 1962, lunch-counter sit-ins and freedom rides tested the segregated South. And in 1963, 250,000 marched on Washington for equality and jobs and fair pay.

John gave a keynote speech.

He put it straight:

"Wake up, America!

. . . We will not and cannot be patient."

Martin told the world,

"I have a dream."

In 1964 came Freedom Summer.
Registering Black folks to vote.
Getting them to the ballot box.

In 1965 peace believers marched
over the Edmund Pettus Bridge,
still fighting for that precious right to vote.

But halfway across

came racism's pounding reign.

Thunderous beatings to John's head.

Billy clubs — *bam!*

Skull cracking — *slam!*

Tear *g a a a a a s s s* . . .

Pepper *s p r a a a a a y y y y y* . . .

Seeing stars explode in broad daylight.

Then . . . not seeing.

Blinded . . . blacked out.

Broken bones.

Choked.

John's faith was tested by scars,

slow to heal on the way to change.

John and Martin stayed strong.

Stayed proud.

Brother-friends.

Together.

Forever.

Then came April 4, 1968.

That heartbreaking day

when Martin rose,

escaping to a place

where hatred doesn't live.

Crossing heaven's bridge

to the other side of bigotry.

Rising to a higher love.

On the shoulders of Saints and Angels:

Harriet, Frederick, Sojourner, DuBois . . .

John Lewis knew he and other makers of

Good Trouble

were left to carry on Martin's dream for peace.

To stitch the seams

of his legacy.

Through the years,
legacy's threads weave on,
stitching in the hopes of Tybre Faw.
Quilted patches of bright promise.

Tybre — bold.

Tybre — more ready than ever.

Tybre — wide-awake
during the seven-hour car trip to Selma,
where John Lewis,
the congressman,
prepares for his memory-march
across the Edmund Pettus Bridge.

Tybre waits
at the back door
of the Brown Chapel AME Church
hoping to meet the fighting-for-freedom,
peace-seeking giant,
Congressman John.

Tybre wishes.
     Tybre prays.
          Tybre waits.
               Tybre stays.
Stands straight and proud.
Heart beating loud.
Hours . . . and hours . . . and hours . . .
Pressed shirt. Necktie.
New shoes, laced tight.
Holding his sign of the times:

Thank you Rep. John Lewis.

You have shown me

how to have courage.

Then — can it truly be?
Yes, here — really here. . . .
A beautiful miracle.

Good Trouble.

Shake . . . shake . . . shaking,
Tybre Faw
is shaking
John Lewis's hand!

They talk. They hug.
Tybre trembles
from the deep-down knowing
that his dream has come true!

Right then, at that spot,
Congressman John
invites Tybre,
who has come all the way
from Tennessee,
to make that trip across
the Edmund Pettus Bridge . . .
. . . walking
. . . next to him!

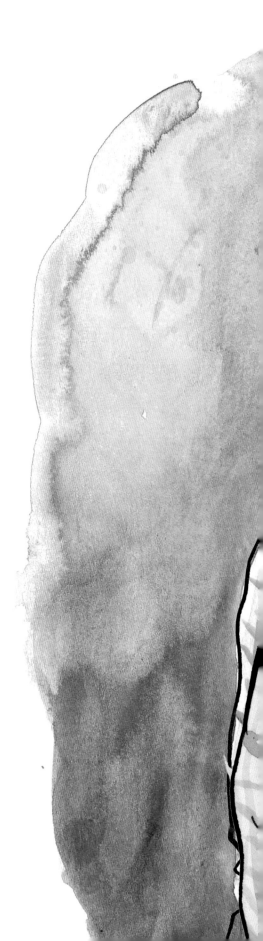

As the new friends walk,

they rise on the wings

of every "Wade in the Water"

that has crossed that bridge before,

and whose echo still whispers a sweet refrain.

Praises be, people!

Praises be!

Together, Tybre Faw

and Congressman John Lewis

bridge the legacy

that has spanned

from Jim Crow's screech

    to "I Have a Dream"

        and to Black Lives Matter.

Yes, they do.

John and Tybre flutter

up, up, up,

straight to the heart and soul of

"Lift Ev'ry Voice and Sing."

There are those who believe

that, deep down,

Congressman John knew he needed a kid

with brand-new shoes.

And sturdy laces, tied tight for walking ahead.

Ready — to take the next steps on freedom's journey.

Ready — to follow in legacy's footsteps by leading
with his own brave feet.

Ready — to reach.

And on the sad, sad day,

when heaven's cloak called John home.

When Martin, who had risen to the other side,

gave an up-nod

to his brother-friend.

When the world said goodbye to the crusader
named Good Trouble.

When Congressman John Robert Lewis was laid to rest,

Tybre Faw stepped up.

Stood tall.

Spoke.

From the Ebenezer Baptist Church,
where Martin had his pulpit,
Tybre delivers his hero's favorite poem,

"Invictus."

Brings those words ahead
like the sun rising on a bright horizon.
Yes, Tybre does.

Speaks — about Courage.

Speaks — about Strength.

Speaks — about the Determination
of moving past doubt.

"Invictus." All about being
the master of your fate.

Now is Tybre's time
to celebrate the man
whose past led to now.
Yes, Tybre's time has come
to pay his respects while the world pays attention.
Listening and learning from those still on the road.
And trusting that we can
open a world of possible.

On that same day,
President Obama celebrates possibility's truth:

Because of you, John Lewis, I stand here today.

Tybre from Tennessee, he knows it, too.

Because of you, John Lewis, we shall not be moved.
Because of you, John, we can all look to the sky.
We can all rise up. We all can fly.

Do you see it up there, the wide-wide blue?
Because of *you* . . . and *you* . . . and *you* . . .
  We will lace new shoes,
    cross big bridges,
      wake up, wish,

        and march

          toward a brighter

            tomorrow.

TWO JOURNEYS.

JOHN ROBERT LEWIS was a man who changed the world. He was an activist, an orator, a crusader, and a leader. Born February 21, 1940, John grew up near Troy, Alabama, where he experienced the unfair treatment of Black people. This came as the result of over 150 years of discrimination — as well as from the Jim Crow laws that denied African Americans basic human rights. These laws had been practiced for nearly a hundred years. And they turned into a system of separation that dictated every aspect of life. John was a teenager when he first heard Martin Luther King, Jr. speak on the radio. Inspired by King's insightful words, John later wrote King a letter, asking advice about being denied admission to Troy State University in Alabama. Dr. King invited John to meet him, and the two became friends. Martin called John "the boy from Troy."

John was ordained as a Baptist minister and moved listeners with his powerful sermons and speeches. He was committed to gaining equality through nonviolence. In 1961, in the early days of his activism, he participated in freedom rides, bus trips through the segregated South that included Black and White passengers who, by riding together, challenged the Jim Crow system of segregated interstate buses and bus terminals. Even though John and other young activists were protesting peacefully, they were beaten by angry mobs and arrested by police.

John became chairman of the Student Nonviolent Coordinating Committee (SNCC), a group of young people who organized sit-ins and other peaceful protests. John's courageous civil rights work continued, and he got into "good trouble" — doing what was necessary to advance the cause of equality by refusing to back down whenever people challenged him to stop.

On August 28, 1963, John marched with Dr. King as a member of the "Big Six," an important group of civil rights influencers leading the protest's procession. And when he spoke at the March on Washington for Jobs and Freedom, he gained national recognition as a young activist who would help lead the movement forward. Like many brave leaders, John was met with resistance. By then, he had been arrested forty times for standing up to injustice.

When he was twenty-three years old, John led more than six hundred marchers in a peaceful, orderly protest across the Edmund Pettus Bridge in Selma, Alabama, to demonstrate the urgent need for voting rights. Soon after the march began, state troopers attacked the demonstrators in a brutal confrontation that came to be called "Bloody Sunday." Over fifty marchers were hospitalized. And the troopers fractured John's skull, leaving scars that he would have for the rest of his life.

ONE DREAM.

John went on to become a congressman and continued his work as a social justice crusader who advocated on behalf of Black people, women, children, and the LGBTQIA+ community. As part of his ongoing stand for civil rights, John made an annual pilgrimage across Selma's Edmund Pettus Bridge to commemorate Bloody Sunday.

John's yearly Edmund Pettus Bridge marches inspired many young people to become activists. One of those young people was Tybre Faw, a ten-year-old from Johnson City, Tennessee. Tybre's interest in history and the civil rights movement began in third grade when his teacher had her students put on a play about Martin Luther King, Jr. This led Tybre to the library to gather books about civil rights leaders. This is how he learned about John Lewis. Lewis's life story and commitment to social justice fascinated Tybre. When Tybre found out that John would be making his annual visit to Selma to commemorate Bloody Sunday, he urged his grandmothers to drive him seven hours from their hometown to meet the congressman. More than anything, Tybre wanted to shake John Lewis's hand. His wish came true in ways he never could have expected.

After a moving and magical meeting with the congressman, and joining him for the walk across the Edmund Pettus Bridge on that day in 2018, Tybre stayed friends with John. Tybre quickly dove into activism. He marched for school safety, human rights, immigrant equality, and any other cause he believed was worth fighting for. Tybre joined John again on March 24, 2018, in Atlanta for the March for Our Lives, and in 2019 and 2020, John again invited Tybre to walk across the Edmund Pettus Bridge as part of his annual commemoration.

In February 2020, Tybre called John to wish him a happy birthday. The congressman had been diagnosed with cancer and didn't know if he would make it to the annual Selma march a month later. Fortunately, John did attend the march. So did Tybre. It was the last time the two of them would see each other. Congressman John Lewis died on July 17, 2020.

The congressman's funeral took place on July 30, 2020, at Atlanta's Ebenzer Baptist Church, the church where Martin Luther King, Jr. had been a minister. Tybre, now twelve years old, was invited to recite the congressman's favorite poem, "Invictus," by William Ernest Henley.

Tybre finished by saying, "John Lewis was my hero, my friend. Let's honor him by getting in good trouble."

TIME LINE OF THE LIFE

FEBRUARY 21, 1940: John Robert Lewis is born, one of ten children, near Troy, Alabama. He was the son of Black sharecroppers and great-grandson of a slave.

1951: When John is bused to middle school eight miles from home, he sees the realities of segregation in the South, including separate drinking fountains for Black people. This same year, during a visit to relatives in upstate New York, John experiences living in an integrated community, and gets a glimmer of hope for an equitable future.

MAY 17, 1954: The *Brown v. Board of Education* ruling brings an expectation that schools will be instantly integrated. John is disappointed when this doesn't happen.

EARLY 1955: John listens to Martin Luther King, Jr.'s "Paul's Letter to American Christians" radio broadcast. John is riveted by the speech, and instantly becomes an admirer of Martin's beliefs.

AUGUST 1955: Fourteen-year-old Emmett Till is brutally murdered for saying "Bye, Baby," to a White store clerk in Money, Mississippi. Lewis was profoundly affected.

DECEMBER 1, 1955: Rosa Parks takes bold action by refusing to give up her seat on a segregated bus, igniting the Montgomery Bus Boycott. This sparks John's interest in civil rights activism. The boycott lasts one year.

FALL 1956: John is accepted as a student at the American Baptist Theological Seminary (ABT) in Nashville, Tennessee.

FALL 1957: John applies to Troy State University. Because he's Black, his application is ignored. When John writes to Martin Luther King, Jr. for advice, Martin invites him to come to Montgomery to speak face-to-face. Martin encourages John to fight for his rights by trying to desegregate Troy State. Afraid for their son's safety, John's parents won't let him pursue this plan. He respects their wishes but vows to get involved with civil rights in other ways.

1960–1962: John participates in sit-ins, mass meetings, and the freedom rides of 1961 that tested racial segregation in the South. (In February 1960, John was arrested for the first of at least forty-five times for his civil rights activities.)

SPRING 1963: John serves as chairman of the Student Nonviolent Coordinating Committee (SNCC). He helps register Black people to vote in Selma, Alabama.

AUGUST 28, 1963: At the March on Washington, which is attended by around 250,000 people, John Lewis delivers a speech that gave him national recognition. There, Martin Luther King, Jr. delivers his historic "I Have a Dream" speech. The march raises national awareness for the eventual passage of the Civil Rights Act of 1964 and the Voting Rights Act of 1965.

MARCH 7, 1965: John is beaten by an Alabama state trooper while attempting to lead an estimated six hundred voting rights marchers out of Selma on the way to Montgomery. The violent confrontation is referred to as Bloody Sunday. John spends two days in a hospital. Around fifty-eight others were injured.

MARCH 21–25, 1965: John and thousands of others protest during the Selma-to-Montgomery voting rights march.

OF REP. JOHN LEWIS

AUGUST 1965: President Lyndon B. Johnson signs the Voting Rights Act of 1965. (Although much work is still needed to end voter suppression.)

1971: John oversees the Voter Education Project, a program of the Southern Regional Council.

NOVEMBER 4, 1986: John is elected to Congress, representing Georgia's Fifth Congressional District, which includes much of Atlanta. He's re-elected sixteen times and is called "The Conscience of Congress."

2001: John receives the John F. Kennedy Profile in Courage Award for Lifetime Achievement.

2011: President Barack Obama presents John with the Presidential Medal of Freedom, the nation's highest civilian honor.

MARCH 8, 2015: John joins President Obama, former President George W. Bush, and thousands of others in Selma at the commemoration of the fiftieth anniversary of Bloody Sunday.

JULY 17, 2020: Lewis dies of pancreatic cancer at the age of eighty.

JULY 27, 2020: One week after Congressman Lewis's death, the Voting Rights Advancement Act (which had passed the US House of Representatives on December 6, 2019) is renamed the "John R. Lewis Voting Rights Act of 2020."

SOURCES AND FURTHER READING   (★RECOMMENDED FOR YOUNG READERS)

In addition to spending time virtually with Tybre and his grandmothers to gather firsthand information about Tybre's friendship/journey with John Lewis, the author also consulted several books, magazines, audio, and audiovisual resources.

BOOKS (SOME AVAILABLE AS AUDIOBOOKS)

★Bolden, Tonya. *MLK: Journey of a King. New York*: Abrams Books for Young Readers, 2006.

Branch, Taylor. *Parting the Waters: America in the King Years* 1954–1963. New York: Simon & Schuster, 1988.

Carson, Clayborne, et.al. *The Eyes on the Prize Civil Rights Reader*. New York: Viking, 1991 (revised edition).

★Kendi, Ibram X., and Jason Reynolds. *Stamped: Racism, Antiracism, and You*. New York: Little, Brown and Company, 2020.

Lewis, John, and Michael Orso. *Walking with the Wind: A Memoir of the Movement*. New York: Simon & Schuster, 1998.

★Lewis, John, and Andrew Aydin. *March* (N. Powell, illus.). Marietta, Georgia: Top Shelf Productions, 2013–2016 (3 volumes).

Meacham, John. *His Truth Is Marching On: John Lewis and the Power of Hope*. New York: Random House, 2020.

PERIODICAL REFERENCE

"John Lewis: 1940–2020." *Time*, August 3–10, 2020.

AUDIO AND AUDIOVISUAL EXPERIENCES

★ *Eyes on the Prize: America's Civil Rights Movement*. PBS, 1986. Seven-volume boxed set.

NEWS COVERAGE OF TYBRE FAW AND JOHN LEWIS

Martin Luther King, Jr.'s "Paul's Letter to American Christians." (This is the sermon/radio broadcast that John Lewis first heard.) *youtube.com.* https://www.youtube.com/watch?v=N-HfpVySfKA

John Lewis's Speech at the 1963 March on Washington. *vimeo.com.* https://vimeo.com/70657416

★ "Tybre Faw Talks about His Relationship with Rep. John Lewis." *youtube.com.* https://www.youtube.com/watch?v=gNRUj-00Cc4

★ "Ten-year-old Tybre Faw Travels 7 Hours to See His Hero, Rep. John Lewis." *youtube.com.* https://www.youtube.com/watch?v=-AfgvtwYNic

★ "12-year-old Recites Poem at John Lewis' Funeral." *youtube.com.* https://www.youtube.com/watch?v=X_BTVTb-1o0

At a 1960 Nashville, Tennessee, lunch counter sit-in, John joined fellow activists. When police officers showed up, they arrested the protesters, who were sitting quietly.

In Anniston, Alabama, a fire bomb ignited a Freedom Rider bus in May 1961. The freedom riders escaped without serious injury. Even with the threat of violence, protesters held to their beliefs in social justice.

John Lewis was arrested many times for participating in nonviolent protests. In the mugshot on the left Lewis is dressed in his best clothing, which protesters often wore as a sign of respect for the movement

In this first march from Selma to Montgomery, John Lewis and Hosea Williams led fellow Black activists to stand up against unfair voting laws. Note the Edmund Pettus Bridge in the background.

John Lewis and other marchers came face-to-face with state troopers as they exited the Edmund Pettus Bridge.

John Lewis lifted a hand, trying to stop the pounding blows, as an Alabama state trooper swung his club at Lewis's head during this march that came to be known as "Bloody Sunday."

Martin Luther King, Jr. (center) and John Lewis (far left) joined arms with other leaders of the movement at the March on Washington.

At the March on Washington, John gave a rousing and powerful speech. He told the world the time had come for change.